SMOKEY AND

MW01272948

George D. Amiotte

Platoon CMDR,
Combined Action Platoon 1

Landing Zone Publishing

Landing Zone Publishing

Landing Zone Publishing
landingzonepublishing@gmail.com

Library of Congress Cataloging-in-Publication Data
Amiotte, George D.
Smokey and His Squad of Fruit Loops
p. cm
ISBN — 9781729507681

Printed in the United States of America

DEDICATED TO

3rd Recon Medal of Honor Recipients
L. Cpl. Richard A. (Tex) Anderson
Lt. Frank S. Reasoner
PFC Robert Jenkins
2 Lt. Terrence Graves

All 3rd Recon Members declared KIA and MIA

This is a story based on experiences during my 2nd, and last, combat tour of duty in the Tam Ky Province, Republic of South Vietnam I was assigned to the 3rd Marine Amphibious Force, Combined Action Group, 1969-70.

I had previously trained Hmong militia groups so the Marine Corps decided I should train South Vietnamese troops... on the job. Twelve of these were boys, ages 10-14. I called them my Fruitloops. They were my little warriors and they helped me begin to heal from the trauma of war

So it is with deep respect and love that I honor the children of the Vietnam War, so many years later, so many tears later. I continue to heal . I still cry and feel sorrow for what we experienced together.

My Fruitloops I honor you by telling your story because I can tell it now. You're no longer part of my wounded past. I celebrate your courage, especially those little boy soldiers that fought alongside of me.

For all my relations.

Baby Buddha
Incident #11

It was 1969. I was 22 years old and leaving the Pine Ridge Reservation in South Dakota to return to Vietnam. It was my second tour of duty with the United States Marine Corps' 3rd Division, Fleet Marine Force. My previous tour of duty was with the 3rd Recon Battalion. I departed the States in hopes of being reassigned to a Recon outfit up North. This was not to be the case. As I landed and entered the terminal in Da Nang, Republic of South Vietnam, two E-5 Marines approached me and cried out, "Sgt. Amiotte! We are from the Combined Action Group (CAG,) we have your new orders.... f***ed!" Those orders read: George D. Amiotte transferred to the Combined Action Program, China Beach Da Nang RSV.

The CAG Program fell under the hospice of the Phoenix Program whose mission was the pacification of the Vietnamese civilian population. We were to win the hearts and minds of the Vietnamese people. *I wasn't a Mud Marine*, I had been a Recon Marine!! Not anymore, not with these orders! We were to accomplish our mission by letting the South Vietnamese begin defending their own villages. A small number of U.S. Marines are assigned to rural areas and tasked with training local South Vietnamese Units while providing access to Artillery, Air, and Medivac services provided by the United States military. Word in the Ranks, was USMC CAG Marines don't last long in the Villages, they either become Wounded In Action or Killed In Action. Plus the fact that the South Vietnamese fighting units aren't exactly known for their fighting abilities. When it came down to a fire fight, the South Vietnamese had Jackrabbit blood. They ran!! President Nixon, or rather "Dirty Dick," was pulling out of Viet Nam and the CAG Program was one of the strategies developed to achieve Peace with Honor.

I soon found myself attending a four-week training program with the Combined Action Group right there in China Beach, Da Nang RSV. It was a refresher course for calling in Artillery, Fixed Wing and refreshing basic support Communication Skills. As a Sgt. E5, I knew I would command a full platoon, someplace out there in what reminded me of "Indian Country" back home. I did not like this assignment! After graduating the refresher course, I was assigned to 1st CAG out of Chu Lai, then to an outpost near the Pineapple Forest, a staging area for the North Vietnamese Army heading South. My Area of Operation (AO) extended into the southern end of this quadrant. I was assigned a Fire Team of Marines, one squad of South Vietnam Army (ARVNS,) one squad of Viet Lops (semi-trained 17-18 year old boys,) and a squad of local militia made up of the youngest men of the villages, they were merely children. My squad of boys ranged in age from 11 to 16 years old. All these young "men" were dressed in camo and carried M-1 Carbines and M-16 rifles. They appeared as regular combat soldiers except being mere children and all barefoot. I named them my Fruit Loops Squad and gave them all American Indian names; Crazy Horse, Geronimo, Red Cloud, Sitting Water Buffalo, Cochise, Osceola, Dull Knife. I never went anywhere without three or four of My Fruit Loops trailing me, seeing to my comfort and care. During the down time of a Patrol I inevitably had a pair of little brown hands giving me a rub down, or cutting my hair soon upon sitting or squatting on the ground. Cochise had a pair of hand-held clippers and was always trimming and grooming the troops, regardless of where we were. They would embed razor blades in slivers of bamboo and shave my ears, eye brows, nasal areas. I told myself that I shouldn't get close to these kids 'cause if they got hurt or killed, I would pay for it later with grief and the bittersweet memories left imprinted on me. I knew about loss. I had lost a few buddies up North with Recon, and it was always hard losing a friend. After awhile you don't make friends, the thought of getting close to anyone escaped me forever!

Though I wasn't fluent, I spoke Vietnamese and some French so I could communicate with just about everybody I ran across, even the elderly ladies at the Market! The Vietnamese seemed to like to hear me speak because of my accent and my pronunciation of their words was entertaining to them. They would laugh and teach me the correct way to say the words I had misspoken. I must have been quite comical to them at times!

It surprised me to learn that the Vietnamese knew quite a bit about American Indians, though they thought that we were still being chased around the country by the Calvary! And we live in tipis made of buffalo hide. They were most interested in my lifestyle back home on the reservation. I shared all kinds of stories from my boyhood of horse ranching, hunting deer and elk in the Black Hills of Dakota, and using a slingshot for "self defense" in the village.

When asked why we wore eagle feathers in our hair I explained that each feather worn represents a deed of honor. Within 1 month after I was there, my Fruit Loops and some of the Neo Quans began wearing chicken and duck feathers tucked in their hats and helmets. I called them My Feather heads. I never lost sight that nobody back home would believe that little boys are fighting this war.

In the hamlet of Phu Tra #1 was a Cao Dae Buddhist temple. There was one monk named Lab Sang living as a caretaker in the temple and chanting Gongyo (prayers to the Lord Buddha,) a mantra chanted each day, sunrise and sunset. One morning in the temple I sang my personal warrior song, it echoed through the temple, I thought it sounded cool vibrating off the walls. Apparently it wasn't cool with the chickens who cackled and squawked in protest. Lab Sang thought he'd heard that melody long before it was sung in the temple that day and expected somebody would arrive to sing it there one day. We had a special friendship that has had deep impact and today remains a powerful influence upon my life.

My interest in Buddhism was born there in Phu Tra #1. When I asked Lab Sang why as a Monk that he was not actively training young sages/interns to continue the life cycle of the temple, he stated that they weren't available to him because I had them! He said that this present time in the cycle of life was out of balance and that "War" claimed his young men. He stated that he was the last Monk and that the jungle would reclaim the temple as told within the Gongyo mantra. Change is the only constant in the Universe.

One of our primary duties was to sweep the road with mine detectors every morning and then run day patrols out in the rice paddies. We had no singular position that we stayed in. Our patrol went from village to village and stayed for only one night. We ran night ambushes on all the paths and back trails in our AO. We took our orders from Battalion and most of the time they allowed us to do our own thing as long as they knew where we were. I would go into each village in advance of the troops and pay respects to the hamlet Chief. I shared tea with him before telling him we would be his guests for the evening.

Troops in the villages draw attention from the NVA; attention like mortar fire and booby traps in the morning. Everything we owned we carried on our backs. We carried a cache of weapons around with us, two M-60 machine guns with ammo, one 60mm mortar and it's ammo, and our small arms, M-16s and M-1 carbines. My Vietnamese counterpart was named Sgt.. Su (Trunksie) and he spoke English pretty fluently but chose to speak to me in French so none of the young Vietnamese troops could understand what he was saying. He had been in the Army for 11 years and came from this region of Tam Ky Province. He carried an old Colt six shooter on his hip. I called him "Cowboy," we got along very well. The troops listen to each of us with equal respect. Trunksie managed the Viet Lops and I managed the Marines.

When a Neo Quan tripped a booby trap I received a small piece of shrapnel that pierced my right thigh and right testicle. The Fruit Loop squad teased me about the wound and said that they would look for my right testicle every time they went out on patrol. I promised whoever found my testicle, that I would give them a carton of Salem cigarettes. After every patrol a Neo Quan would show me a dead mouse, dog turd, tree nuts, even a head of a duck, and ask me if that was my testicle. The kids would say "show us where you got wounded!!" Or, "did you find your balls yet!?" I told them not to be calling my Captain, "Captain Dip Shit," when he comes out, only I can call him Captain Dip Shit. "Ohhh, You mean Captain Shit for Brains. Captain Shit Bird? When your Captain Dip Shit comes here we tell him you number 1 Jarhead, pay him more money! No more shit jobs! He want to use flush toilet. He miss his round eye girl."There was a village, Phu Tri 3, out near the West end of my AO. It looked like a painting and sat out on an island, surrounded by rice paddies. It was a hamlet of only 5 families. The village hamlet Chief was a crusty old guy and I loved listening to his war stories of kicking the French out of Viet Nam. The Chief had a grandson only 7 months old. I loved to hold him. The baby had a Buddha crop of hair on his forehead and wore a jade Buddha around his neck on a gold chain. I felt so safe when holding this child, as long as I held this child nothing could hurt me. How could the creator harm such a loving child as this? I cherished my visits with the Chieftain and his grandson. I called the small child Little Buddha.

About a month before I was due to rotate, I was in the city of Tam Ky when I got a call that a team from my CAG was in contact with NVA (North Vietnam Army) and I should return to my Unit post haste. From the radio conversations I heard in transit, I understood that Phu Tri 3 was involved. When I arrived the fire fight had ended. Our troops had ambushed NVA troops in the hamlet and there was a shoot out. One South Vietnamese trooper KIA and three NVA KIA. The Chief and his baby grandson were caught in the crossfire and killed. Sgt.. Su, "Cowboy" met me on the trail to the hamlet. He knew of my friendship with the

Chief and Little Buddha, He said "George" (he never called me George) "please stay here, yes the Papa San is dead and so is Little Buddha. I Sorry. You no...*You no need to see!* Very bad to see. No go!!!" I shoved my friend aside and ran up the trail to the little hamlet. On the tiles of the courtyard lay the Chieftain and his Grandson. Little Buddha was wrapped in a burlap bag and had bled out on the tiles. I picked the lifeless bundle up in my arms and couldn't believe that what I was holding was once the beautiful child sent to me to just hold for a moment and let me know I was alive and that I could love something, someone again. The Creator had given me something more than I thought that I could handle. I buried my face in that bloody bundle and cried, I don't know how long I sat there holding Little Buddha, what blood he had left in his little body drained out on me. I could feel it dripping onto my lap. One of the Neo Quans asked me for the baby. I couldn't let him go. My Fruit Loops were scared by my grief and appearance, all covered in the blood of Little Buddha. I was immediately struck by a memory from the past, a warning about not getting too close.

Sgt. Su knelt before me and put his hands on mine. "George, I know this is painful for you. Baby come here for little while in life. He bring happiness to all who know him. Now Baby gone, bring sadness to all. Baby must continue his journey to the Spirit World. It is good to mourn his life, your grief shows your love for him, now he must be released." I surrendered the corpse to Sgt. Su and he gave the lifeless child to a family member. Sgt. Su took a canteen of water and held my head back and poured the water on my face to wash away the blood, I felt the loving touch of an older brother and I felt safe and secure again. He said to me, "That love you showed for Little Buddha is alive in the universe and you and he will certainly meet again in another lifetime. In his dreams he will know you as a warrior from another land that came to help his people. There were three Spirits with you this day, Your Father, Your creator! The Chieftain, and Little Buddha. It was they that held you together. You can look at this day as a very bad day in your life or you can look upon it a beautiful experience and a blessing. You make the choice." Su handed me the little jade Buddha necklace that the baby had worn, he said the family wanted me to have it. It is wrapped in my sacred medicine bundle to this day.

As a civilian I worked as a Physician's Assistant for much of my adult life and mostly in Indian Country. Little fat babies always receive a warm welcome and soothe the PTSD within me. All because of Little Buddha.

Later in life, my daughter Lalena gifted me with a beautiful Granddaughter named Mary Jane, who is wise beyond her years and a healer at heart. When her little hands are massaging my back and shoulders, as she so often does, I am reminded of my little Fruit Loop Squad, and Little Buddha who guards sacred fireflies in that quiet Asian night. The last Monk and my Fruit Loops.

– to be continued....

Receiving the Bronze Star Feb. '70

George Duane Amiotte was born December 17, 1947 on the Pine Ridge (Indian) Reservation near the Black Hills of South Dakota. An Oglala Sioux, Amiotte grew up attending St. Stephan Catholic School on the reservation. He enlisted in the United States Marine Corps in 1965 at the age of 17. After two tours of duty in Viet Nam, and one to the Philippines, he was honorably discharged in 1970. His training included Schools: Recon, Scuba, Scout Sniper, Jungle Environmental Survival Training, Combined Action Group Training, Search and Rescue (body recovery.) Amiotte was awarded the Purple Heart, Bronze Star, and the Vietnamese Cross of Gallantry for his service in the USMC. As a civilian Amiotte graduated from North Dakota School of Medicine in 1973 and became a Physician's Assistant, he contracted as a PA for Indian Health Services and practiced General Medicine until 2006. Aside from his work in Medicine, Amiotte entered the field of Film and Television as a writer, actor, and producer of educational documentaries. His work has been aired on HBO, ABC, NBC, PBS, CANADIAN PBS, and has been installed in many school and university libraries.

After semi-retirement Amiotte now spends his time advocating for Veterans with PTSD. His involvement includes establishing Vet Centers and developing programs to address PTSD patients as well as professionals dealing with patients suffering PTSD which are accomplished through 3-5 day conferences such as Camp Chaparral held in Yakima, WA and The Way of The Warrior held in Custer, SD.

Amiotte resides in the Pacific NW, surrounded by Old Growth forests near the foothills of the Olympic Mountains. He is presently in pre-production of the upcoming documentary OPERATION HEAVEN FIRE: Seeing PTSD Through A Shared Lens As Warriors of the Viet Cong Meet Warriors of the United States In Viet Nam Many Decades Later.

Scuba School
Phillipines - '67

Newly formed Echo Co.
Okinawa - '68

Guard Duty
Phillipines – '66

Aschau Valley – '68

Day Patrol with ARVANS

Hi Mom – '67

Disposing of booby traps.

Weekly hot lunch and re-supply

Rear end Charlie

Cleo the Dog,
Nadine the machine gun.
They both bark!

California dreaming....

Troops of Combined Action Platoon 1

Cpl. Hammer and Leo

Kit Carson Scout, NVA

Duke, KIA
Dec. '69

Lab Sang Rampa
Spiritual Adviser
(he showed me the face of God)

THE WAY OF THE WARRIOR
CONQUERING THE TRAUMA OF POST TRAUMATIC STRESS

The Way of the Warrior is a five day PTSD workshop and expedition blending traditional and non-traditional practices for diagnosing and treating symptoms of combat-related PTSD. The workshop takes place in an outdoor setting such as Camp Legacy in Salem, Or and Camp Chaparral in Yakima, WA. The program is uniquely suited to both the bearer of PTSD and the special care provider. Lectures, role playing and group discussion are utilized as educational activities. Methodology addresses the emotional, physical and spiritual wounds of war. Techniques address wounds incurred by close family and how these wounds transfer cross gene-rationally. The intended outcome is primarily for the veteran to develop a better understanding of their own form of PTSD, and secondarily for the Special Care facilitator to better understand the internal components of those who suffer combat-related PTSD while honing the skill of empathy through the experience. CEUs are granted to Special Care participants. Certificates are granted to PTSD participants as they complete each level of the quarterly offerings designed to build on expand as in stair-step fashion.

The Way Of The Warrior Team consists of psychology and medical professionals, alternative healers, and are led by George Amiotte, all of whom are combat veterans. Their shared experience embraces camaraderie and humor as tough issues and resolutions are presented.

"Mr. Amiotte's presentation on the anatomy of PTSD was an educational experience. He speaks of information that hasn't been published yet."

--Camp Chaparral Attendee

Mr. Amiotte masterfully wove humor into his presentations, his alternative approaches to dealing with PTSD should be a prerequisite for any mental health worker who intends to work for the VA. He is light years ahead of the VA's approach to PTSD treatment. When I wasn't laughing I was crying, bring Kleenex!

--Camp Chaparral Attendee

"Mr. Amiotte opened some doors for me to effectively deal with my own PTSD, I now have a foundation to work from whereas before the workshop I only had my own fear."

--Camp Chaparral Attendee

For more information:
Heaven Fire Productions
PO Box 909
Hoodsport, WA 98548

Landing Zone Publishing

Made in the USA
Middletown, DE
26 August 2022